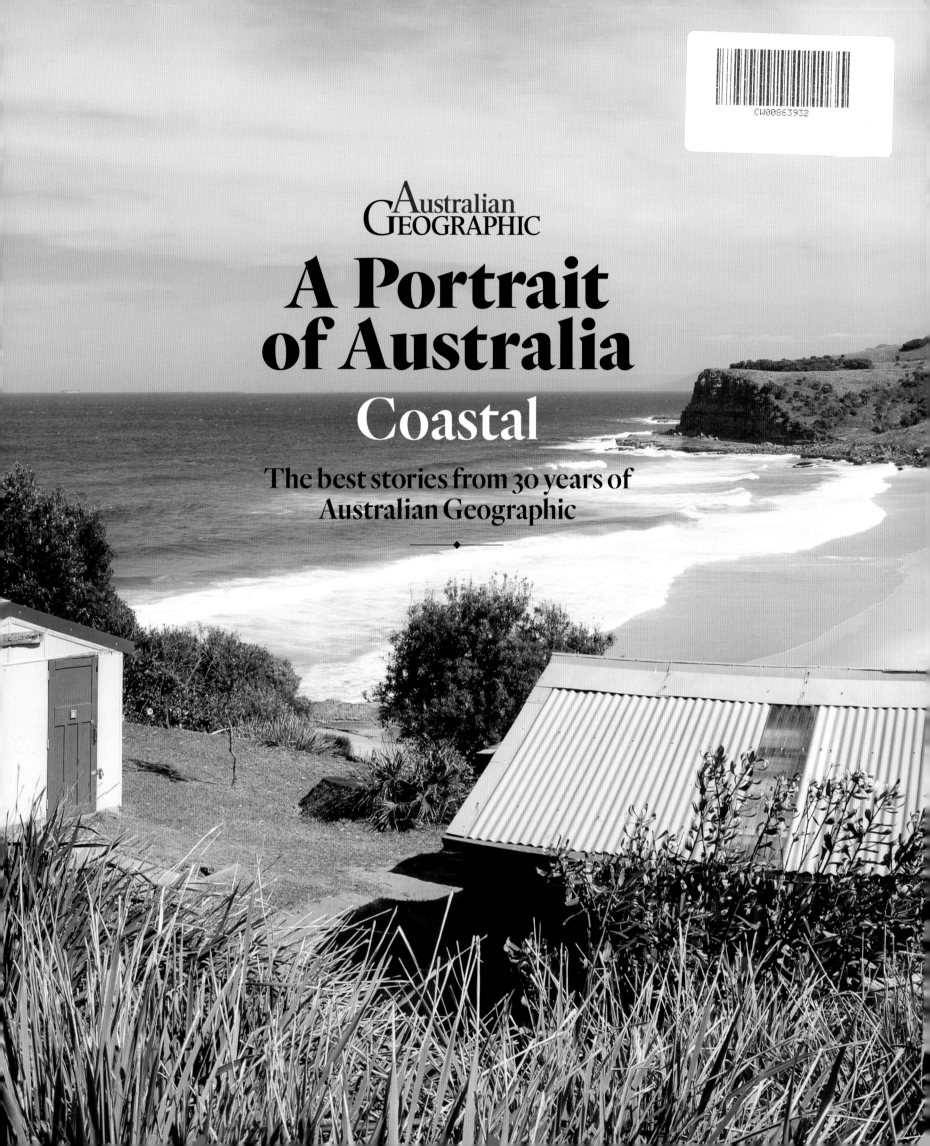

Australian GEOGRAPHIC

A Portrait of Australia

Coastal

The best stories from 30 years of
Australian Geographic

Previous page
The hills above Burning Palms in the
Royal National Park are decorated with
28 mismatched, NSW heritage-listed shacks.
Photo by Andrew Gregory.

This page
Visitors come face to face with an Australian
sea lion colony via a boardwalk at Seal Bay
Conservation Park, on Kangaroo Island's
south coast.
Photo by Bill Bachman.

Contents

Aboriginal and Torres Strait Islander people are advised that this book may contain images and names of people who have died.

The stories included date from 1986-2016 and may reflect the times in which they were written. They may also contain facts, figures and values that were correct at the time of original publication.

Australian GEOGRAPHIC

VOL 1 • NO 1
JAN • MAR 1986

'$6.50

DICK SMITH'S JOURNAL OF DISCOVERY AND ADVENTURE

FIRST ISSUE
Collector's Edition

- LASSETER'S LOST REEF: All of the Evidence
- HALLEY'S COMET RETURNS • MOREE • FRESHWATER EELS
- PROJECT BLIZZARD – MAWSON'S ICY LEGACY • AUSSAT

Watch for our exciting documentary PROJECT BLIZZARD on ABC TV

Foreword

by **Dick Smith** AC, founder of AUSTRALIAN GEOGRAPHIC
and patron of the Australian Geographic Society.

———

WHEN I PUBLISHED the first issue of AUSTRALIAN GEOGRAPHIC in January 1986, I realised a long-held dream of launching a magazine that would present a positive view of Australia, and encourage a spirit of adventure among its citizens young and old.

It wasn't a fashionable notion at the time and certainly there were those who thought such a venture was bound to fail. But I was motivated by a need to share my passion for Australia's remote places and the kinds of people who live there. I was fortunate to have grown up in the 1950s, a time in which I could push the boundaries and give full vent to my natural inclination to venture beyond my comfort zone. It's much harder for modern parents to be able to let their children run free in the way we did back then and I realise now how lucky we were.

I gained an appreciation of and respect for those hard-to-get-to places that lie beyond the big cities and, later in my career when I became a pilot, my wife Pip and I were able to enjoy the freedom and privilege of exploring this vast, amazing continent from shore to shore by air, meeting many memorable people. However wild and beautiful the landscapes that we discovered, it was inevitably the characters we met along the way who left an indelible impression on us both. There's often a kind of disarming honesty, directness and wit with country people that compels you to cast off your city polish, muck in and get on with it, and it's this that draws me back out there whenever possible.

The AUSTRALIAN GEOGRAPHIC journal gave me the opportunity to present a face of Australia that was generally ignored by mainstream media at that time, and you responded in your hundreds of thousands. Over 30 years, the journal has remained committed to seeking out and presenting original

The cover of the launch issue of the journal in January 1986 with 'Banjo' the platypus (opposite). Dick Smith pictured in front of the legendary Birdsville Pub (left).
Photo by Pip Smith.

———

stories about real Australians. We have looked wistfully at their enduring sense of community as we witness the increasing isolation that haunts our overcrowded cities. We have sympathised with their challenges and setbacks but, always, we have respected and admired their lives.

I'm so delighted to be able to revisit some of the fine writing and beautiful photography with which we have lovingly communicated these narratives in this special celebratory series that's been compiled to mark 30 years of AUSTRALIAN GEOGRAPHIC. The journalists and photographers whose work features in AUSTRALIAN GEOGRAPHIC are among the top people in their fields and their efforts stand the test of time as you will see as you leaf through these pages.

I'm sure those of you who remember these stories the first time around will enjoy revisiting them and, if you are reading them for the first time, I hope that this collection goes some way towards creating that elusive portrait of Australia. As you'll see, we have many faces, but certain recurrent characteristics of resourcefulness, courage in adversity, community spirit and a gritty kind of humour are traits that we can all aspire to. ■

Introduction

LIKE ANY NATION, Australia is hard to sum up in simple terms. To attempt to do so is to render a grand disservice to the complexity of human communities – those myriad groupings of people based on shared ethnicities or beliefs, interests, family ties or numerous other reasons that people come together or identify with one another.

It is easier, perhaps, to discern a few common traits that distinguish a particular community. Therefore, when we pause to ponder what makes a fair dinkum Aussie, there are certain archetypes, often honed in popular culture, who readily spring to mind. Like all archetypes, however, they run the risk of evolving into stereotypes or worse, caricatures. The likes of Mick 'Crocodile' Dundee and Dame Edna help us recognise and enjoy some of our more entertaining national characteristics, however the real attributes that identify and unite us are shifting, complex and harder to define.

Looking back through 30 years of the AUSTRALIAN GEOGRAPHIC journal, with its unparalleled coverage of Australia's land, nature and people, a version of our national identity does emerge. The people whose lives have been brought sharply into focus across its glossy, colour-saturated pages have tended to live beyond the security of the big metropolises. They dwell in places where the vagaries of weather and climate dictate the fortunes of those willing to try their luck. If we are influenced by our physical environment, then these Australians have been forged by a monumental and often hostile landscape, whether they arrived in modern times, or have lived here for millennia.

They include the farming folk who live in the bush – that hard-to-define buffer that separates the hot, dry, arid centre of Australia from the cooler coastal fringe where most of us live. It defies a precise geographical definition but, like the outback, we know it when we see it. It is where our crops are grown and herds of sheep and cattle graze unperturbed by the mobs of kangaroos and wombats foraging alongside. Here long, straight roads stretch away to the vanishing point punctuated at uneven intervals by small towns whose populations can sometimes be counted in single digits. From this axis of town and country, Australia's early economic success sprang as resilience, resourcefulness and innovation transformed marginal lands into breadbaskets and unearthed untold mineral riches beneath.

Venture further into Australia's heart, and bush eventually turns to outback, where red dirt meets big blue skies and people are few and far between. It took guts, endurance and perseverance to survive and thrive in these harsh, unforgiving landscapes, whether by the Indigenous occupants or those who arrived later wielding pickaxes or driving huge mobs of cattle to pastures new. It is still a tough place to live and, with a population density of less than 0.1 person per square kilometre, it is one of the most sparsely populated regions on the planet.

These epic landscapes epitomise Australia, but there is a third geographical feature that completes the trifecta: our 60,000km of coastline and islands. While the majority of us live close to the ocean, we are concentrated in pockets close to cities or along the developed east coast. The rest of our shoreline stretches for hundreds of kilometres, sometimes with barely a human footprint or tyre track to betray our presence. Strung

It's a feast fit for a king. Brothers Grant (left) and Paul Jordan display a catch of southern rock lobster, part of the bounty that has secured King Island's reputation as a virtual food platter in the sea.
Photo by Bill Bachman.

out along this vast coastline and more than 8000 offshore islands, people have learnt to reap the harvest of the ocean or have sought to escape the rat-race and are living in places where rhythms of sea and weather dictate the daily routine.

These landscapes and the people who live there are what inspire us at AUSTRALIAN GEOGRAPHIC. In the generation since we first started despatching writers and photographers across the nation to uncover distant communities, we have travelled widely and spent the time needed to delve below the surface to tell their true stories, unashamedly seeking out the positive angle.

When we started the challenging job of identifying articles for inclusion in this compilation of the best of the first 30 years of AUSTRALIAN GEOGRAPHIC, it became clear that the outstanding achievement of the magazine has been its sensitive portrayal of real Australian people. This collection has become a celebration in words and pictures of their indomitable community spirit, their struggles, passions, livelihoods, skills and the changing times through which they have lived, and many themes and personal attributes recur throughout these pages.

The selected articles have been edited to fit the format of

the series. Each bears the original issue and publication date so that you can go back and read the entire original story if you wish. However, if you do not have copies of those original journals on your bookshelf, all past editions are visible on our website *www.australiangeographic.com.au* under the archive section.

I wish to acknowledge the AUSTRALIAN GEOGRAPHIC editors who have strived to uphold the standards of excellence set by Dick Smith and founding editor Howard Whelan. In the face of massive technological and social change, it is a tribute to all of them that the AUSTRALIAN GEOGRAPHIC journal has maintained its relevance and the quality of its reporting. They are Terri Cowley, Ken Eastwood, Dee Nolan, Ian Connellan and John Pickrell.

I hope that you enjoy this collection of the best stories. There are many more we would have included if space had allowed, but, taken together, we believe this anthology paints a vibrant portrait of an Australia of which we can all be proud. ■

BY CHRISSIE GOLDRICK, EDITOR-IN-CHIEF,
AUSTRALIAN GEOGRAPHIC

Coastal

"Water defines character as much as does the land itself...the balance between beach and forest, comfort and challenge, wilderness and civilisation."

————————— **Cape of contrast, page 38**

WITH THREE-QUARTERS of us living within cooee of the coast, it's not surprising that salt water courses through the nation's lifeblood.

The coast is where we head for summer holidays and the source of our sun-bronzed surfer image. It's the launch pad for our $2.2 billion fishing industry and the turbulent barrier that both shields and connects us with the rest of the world.

The coastline of mainland Australia and Tasmania is one of the world's longest at almost 36,000km. It's littered with middens of the shells and bones of sea creatures, telling a story stretching back millennia of prosperous living by our Indigenous peoples. But it's also a long, sad graveyard of shipwrecks that speak of hundreds of years of tragedy for much newer arrivals.

The rest of the world knows us as much for our coastal features as for our legendary Red Centre. Just off Western Australia, the World Heritage-listed Ningaloo Reef plays host to the world's biggest fish – whale sharks that arrive annually without fail on feeding migrations. Our coast is where the 12 Apostles hold a shaky line to the south and the Great Barrier Reef to the east feeds the ocean well beyond our borders with life.

No-one owns any of our 10,700 beaches – from the iconic Bondi in NSW and Bells in Victoria to the stunning arc of sand that hugs Wineglass Bay on Tasmania's Freycinet Peninsula. But most of us each claim at least some possession, whether it's with a spot on a towel in the sun or in a Depression-era beach shack overlooking Australia's oldest national park, the Royal, south of Sydney.

Our country is not only a continent. Our coastline links us to more than 8000 islands that also make up Australia. They range from the little known South Cumberland Islands, down the coast from the better-known Whitsundays, off Queensland; to the tropical Indigenous paradise of Groote Eylandt, Australia's third largest island, lying within the Anindilyakwa Indigenous Protected Area, in the Gulf of Carpentaria, off the Northern Territory. To the south, Bass Strait's wild waters deliver a living based on giant seaweed to some residents of King Island, off Tasmania's north-western tip.

Much of Australia's vast inland is connected with the coast, via the mighty Murray, our longest river. This great snake of water finally reaches the coast at the Coorong on South Australia's south-east coast, to trickle into the Great Australian Bight. Vast numbers of birds thrive on the wetlands here. And just like so much of Australia's coast, life ripples and pulses under the influence of the tide. ■

—————
Previous page.

Alan House gathers oyster baskets at Freycinet Marine Farm ready to take them out to the Swan River estuary. See *Beyond the bay* p28. **Photo by Nick Rains.**

Cape of contrast

A roaring 3m swell dumps down onto rocks south of Conto, in WA's Capes Region. Surf as big as 10m can strike offshore here. See p38.
Photo by Andrew Gregory.

The salt-laden, year-round winds that toss the kelp ashore shorten the lives of vehicles. So, showing the ingenuity that's a trait of King Islanders, part-time tour-bus operator and kelp harvester Graeme Stingel turned his rusted Kombi into a woodshed, packing it to the roof with neatly cut tea-tree logs.

Spindrift and surf at his back, islander Tim Robertson sloshes through the shallows of the west coast's British Admiral Beach. Harvesters, or kelpies, have to avoid getting too much sand on the seaweed, because sandy kelp dries slower than clean fronds dragged from rocky shores and may rot on the drying racks.

Kings of kelp

Along King Island's jagged coastline, Bass Strait's turbulent waters rip tough bull kelp from underwater rocks and toss it ashore where it's harvested.

Issue 51 Jul-Sep 1998

TEXT BY **CHRIS VINEY** PHOTOGRAPHY BY **ROB WALLS**

ALL NIGHT the storm howled; a black flood of wind battering the rocky coast. In the morning, ragged lines of foam marched in from the Southern Ocean to beach their energy on the shores of King Island, at Bass Strait's western entrance. Bombarded by the wind-driven spray, I teetered across a mass of shore-cast bull kelp, slipping on the wet, leathery leaves, watching kelp harvester Neil Lewis dragging the end of a steel cable with captive nooses of coloured cord. With hair flying and a broad grin he was enjoying this wild, windy work. "Mate, you wouldn't be dead for quids!" he shouted into the gale.

A dozen metre-long loops were attached to the steel 'dragline' by metal rings. Grabbing a handful of cords, I fumbled with cold, wet fingers to attach simple slipknots to wrist-thick kelp stalks. Neil did the same, and when every noose was securely tied to a stalk, his truck-mounted winch whined into action. The cable wound onto the drum, and a clutch of glistening-black 4m kelp streamers was hauled out of the shallows, over the rocks and onto the tray of Neil's bright-red truck.

Neil slashed through the pliable stalks with a huge knife, tossing them onto the rocks where they joined a stack of others. We pulled the dragline back into the shallows, five times tying on and loading a dozen broken-off kelp plants. After three hours, the tray was piled high with a dripping, sea-reeking load. Neil started the truck and set off on the 2km trip to the Kelp Industries processing plant just south of Currie, the larger of King Island's two towns. There the island's kelp is dried, milled and reduced to a granular form. Most is then exported to Europe where it's ultimately converted into a form used worldwide in thousands of different products and applications – from hair shampoos and cosmetics to processed cheeses and jams.

From small beginnings in the early 1970s, kelping – kelp harvesting – has become a major part of many a King Islander's way of life. It provides full-time employment for only one or two people but part-time work for more than 100 of the 2000 residents, annually adding an estimated $2.5 million [1998 values] to the farming, fishing and tourism-based economy here.

Better known for its cheeses, cream and beef, King Island is surrounded by shallow-growing bull kelp, a macroalga containing particularly high levels of the compound algin. Bass Strait's tumultuous waves and storms regularly tear the plants' holdfasts from the rocks on which they grow, dragging many into marine gullies, where they decay or are eaten by creatures such as abalone. Other detached kelp washes ashore, where it can be legally harvested by the island's 100 licensed 'kelpies'.

Like most kelpies, Graeme Stingel juggles several jobs: as well as carting kelp, he runs a few head of cattle and drives one of the island's tour buses.

"One thing kelp has done for the island is to just about knock off unemployment," he said between chores on his 2.5ha farmlet. "You're never going to make your fortune kelping, but most kelpies like the lifestyle." ∎

Vlamingh Head lighthouse in Cape Range National Park is built from local stone and has been guarding the coast north of Exmouth since 1912.

Ningaloo revealed

With long, empty beaches, glistening turquoise waters and amazing marine wildlife, Ningaloo Reef is attracting a whole new generation of visitors.

Issue 84 Oct -Dec 2006

STORY BY **JAMES WOODFORD**
PHOTOGRAPHY BY **ANDREW GREGORY**

A NYONE WHO SAYS megafauna are extinct has never donned goggles at Ningaloo Reef. I roll off the Zodiac into the water, see a 2m mammal heading towards me and duck-dive down to the seagrass on the sandy bottom to watch nervously as the creature passes within a body length of me. Its whiskered face is so close I can see its chocolate eyes looking into mine. The encounter is so unexpected I feel a flash of fear and wonder if dugongs are dangerous. After just days at Ningaloo, however, I've already learnt the prerequisite for swimming here – put your worries aside. This is the playground of some of the world's largest and most gentle animals.

With a flick of its mermaid tail, the dugong lifts its 400kg bulk to the surface and, after a few minutes, disappears with surprising speed and grace.

The word Ningaloo belongs to the Gnulli people, traditional owners of the coast surrounding WA's North West Cape, and means promontory. Shaped like a beckoning finger, nearly 200km long and jutting into the Indian Ocean, it stretches along the coast between Carnarvon and Exmouth and conjures images of whale sharks, coral, wilderness and adventure.

It is one of Australia's driest landscapes – with a mere 226mm a year of rain and an annual evaporation rate of more than 2.5m. Some years, if there isn't a cyclone, it doesn't $\longrightarrow$

rain at all. On average, the sun shines 320 days out of 365.

Ningaloo is famous not just for its reef, surf breaks and fishing but also soul-destroying winds, white-hot 45°C temperatures and frontier-like feel. The landscape's harshness, swarms of native wasps and bush flies, fine sand that blows into every nook and cranny, and burning sun make its gentler moments seem like epiphanies.

Standing sentinel over the northern reef is Cape Range, a rugged upward fold of limestone packed with fossilised prehistoric marine life including countless perfectly preserved and visible shark teeth embedded in the rock. Inside the boundaries of the surrounding 47,655ha Cape Range system of sinkholes and caves that underpin the peninsula's weathered spine is the oldest evidence of the collection and use of fish, shellfish and crabs by Indigenous Australians – an astonishing 32,000 years.

Ningaloo Reef itself stretches from skyscraper-high military radio antennas outside Exmouth, southwards for almost 300km: the nation's longest fringing coral reef and namesake of the 5218sq.km Ningaloo Marine Park.

Anyone expecting a miniature Great Barrier Reef has come to the wrong place. Instead of rainforest meeting the sea, it's spinifex and sand dunes. Instead of big tourist cities like Cairns and Townsville, the Ningaloo coast has Exmouth – population just 2400. Visitors arriving at Learmonth Airport, 35km south, are as likely to meet a worker en route to an oil rig or a defence official as a backpacker. In fact, upon landing, flight attendants request no photographs for security reasons. Even so, WA Department of Environment and Conservation (DEC) Ningaloo manager, Jennie Cary, says visitor numbers are growing fast. Annual visitation is around 300,000 and increasing annually at 10 per cent.

Jennie has been coming to Ningaloo for more than 30 years, since first visiting with her parents in the days people came for one reason only – to fish for game species like marlin and the prized spangled emperor. Back then no-one swam because Ningaloo's waters were popularly believed to be shark-infested. When swimming did take off in the late '80s, it focused on the whale sharks and they remain the biggest attraction.

"In the '70s, all people did every day at Ningaloo was fish," Jennie says. "Now we're seeing a lot more canoes, kayaks, snorkelling and diving… The name has definitely got out."

Even surfers have begun making pilgrimages to Ningaloo's increasingly famous reef breaks, including those at Lighthouse Bay and Tantabiddi at the marine park's northern reach, and Red Bluff and Gnaraloo – also a mecca for wind and kite surfers – in the south.

Scientists are also teasing out some of Ningaloo's more subtle secrets. In autumn 2006, Australian Institute of Marine Science researchers discovered in the marine park's deeper waters sponge gardens of species thought to be new to science.

Lanky young pilot Rob Connaughton is based at one of the most low-key airport terminals in the country. When not flying, he waits for tourists in a caravan in the middle of a gravel-and-spinifex field 1km from Yardie Homestead on the northern tip of North West Cape. Part of Rob's job is to help skippers and scientists locate whale sharks. The world's biggest fish can reach lengths of 12m, but they glide below the surface and rarely breech, making them almost impossible to see until a boat is virtually on top of them.

Offshore, out of sight on Ningaloo Reef's seaward side, a cruiser loaded with tourists – mostly aged 21-35 years and heralding from Australia, Europe and Japan – is waiting for Rob to take off and pinpoint sharks and manta rays.

We're soon flying over the sand dunes fronting Ningaloo lagoon and heading out to sea. It's a magnificent day – light winds, unbroken blue skies and an ocean so clear the shadow of a boat is cast sharply on the seabed.

At first glance it's hard to believe there's any life at Ningaloo. There are no trees on the shoreline, no freshwater, only the great Indian Ocean meeting the extreme edge of a baked continent. But the Leeuwin Current gives life to the waters here, maintaining a rich flow of warm water and a conveyor belt of nutrients along the WA coast. Every few seconds the sea below our aeroplane boils over as football field-sized schools of fish break the surface and flocks of seabirds swoop to join the feast.

We approach the boat, flying in expanding circles around it and a smudge resembling a half-submerged car comes into view. "There's a manta out here if you want it," Rob says to the skipper. The boat speeds under Rob's guidance towards the pirouetting manta and slows as it gets close. From 500m we watch a rush of people splash into the water and swim towards the manta.

Rob heads south, his neck cricked searching for the creature that sits at the summit of the WA ecotourism food chain. The pressure's on Rob too. From the air whale sharks look almost like tadpoles, he says.

"Their tails are negatively buoyant so they sink down and they have this big flat head. If you see a small one you have to make sure it's spotted not stripy because you do get tiger sharks hanging around here as well."

We're now parallel to the reef and a tadpole-like smudge appears in the water; its motion slow and calm. Rob calls the skipper: he's spotted a whale shark of about 6m, heading towards the north passage.

The boat speeds towards the enormous fish while we fly tight circles directing the skipper until he's 30m – the minimum legal distance – in front of the shark. The tourists jump into the ocean and split into groups each side of the behemoth. After a few minutes, only the strongest swimmers maintain their shark-side vigil and then it dives, disappearing from view.

The reef at Ningaloo is rarely more than a few kilometres offshore and in many places is so close to the beach that children are able wade out to it. This means that anyone with legs, flippers, a boat or kayak can experience the marine park's best corals.

Treading water several kilometres offshore, I note how harsh and desolate the mainland looks. But taking a breath and ducking beneath the chop, I see why Ningaloo was a candidate for World Heritage listing [granted in 2011]. Every dive is different – unique bommies, corals, sea life and underwater topography.

Until about 20 years ago, Coral Bay was a sleepy camping ground between two vast stretches of wilderness coast; a place used by families with tinnies and canvas tents, but things are changing – boats are getting bigger, whiter and shinier. Caravans are now the size of small houses and visitor numbers grow annually. Further north, Exmouth is booming, with a major marina and canal-style housing development under construction.

While whale sharks seem to be holding their own against the rising tide of people, there are concerns about other creatures such as manta rays. "Until now, Ningaloo has been saved by its isolation and protected by its inhospitable environment," explains Murdoch University manta ray researcher Frazer McGregor, who's so passionate about the winged fish he also works as a tour-boat deckhand along the coast. "But how much disturbance can they bear?" ∎

Spent but happy, a group of young surfers recover from the swell and relax outside one of South Era beach's 95 shacks.

Billy Burn, 73, enjoys the solitude of his home away from home; his beach shack at Black Gin Gully above Little Garie Beach in the Royal National Park, NSW.

Places in the heart

Heritage listing has ensured the future of a no-frills Aussie beach experience that's endured since the Great Depression.

Issue 111 Nov-Dec 2012

STORY BY **ERIN O'DWYER** PHOTOGRAPHY BY **ANDREW GREGORY**

IN A REMOTE corner of NSW's Royal National Park, beach huts lie amid the folds and foothills of lush Black Gin Gully, which rises above Little Garie Beach.

"Some shacks were built by the ocean so they could get the view. Others, like ours, are close to the creek," says Billy Burn, 73, whose father-in-law, a miner from nearby Helensburgh, built a shack here in 1942. "It was great when the kids were little. We would fill two buckets with water and bring them back to wash the nappies."

Inside, the shack is filled with 1940s technology: a bright-blue kerosene fridge, a lime-and-cream enamelled kerosene oven, a blackened metho burner and a row of old kerosene lamps hanging from nails.

There's 1950s bric-a-brac, too – a laminex table in sparkling yellow, and carpet tiles on the floor. These days, there are solar panels on the roof too. "The grandkids just come in and flick on the lights," says Billy, smiling. "They don't remember what it used to be like."

There are 143 beach shacks in this section of the park, about 50km south of Sydney: 20 at Little Garie, 95 at South Era and another 28 at Burning Palms. Most date back to the 1930s and '40s, when miners from Helensburgh, at the southern edge of the park, came to the coast looking for a weekend escape. Holidaymakers from Sydney trekked south too: surfers, bush-walkers and families.

During the Great Depression, people lived there out of desperation, surviving on wild rabbits, fish and home-grown vegetables. At the time, pockets of land were still privately owned in the park. Holidaymakers paid two shillings a week to erect tents and rough bark huts. Later, they built permanent cabins, hastily constructed with nails, bits of weatherboard, corrugated iron, planks of driftwood and local stone.

For years, the shacks were at risk of demolition. Some were abandoned, others were deliberately demolished under a controversial National Parks and Wildlife Service (NPWS) policy. A new, five-year licensing arrangement put forward in 2005 prompted the three communities of 'shackies' to challenge the NPWS in court. After mediation in 2006, a 20-year licensing agreement was established.

In April 2012 the shacks were finally listed on the NSW State Heritage Register. The shackies continue to pay rent to the NPWS, but the shacks remain in family ownership.

"Every shack reflects its owner's taste and personality," says Kerry McKenzie, 59, a wedding celebrant from nearby Heathcote. Her father-in-law built a shack at Little Garie in 1946, after visiting the area with the Maroubra Surf Club. He died two years ago and his family members take turns staying at the pretty yellow shack. "To put into words what the place means is extremely difficult," says Kerry. "We call it Garie Fever. Once here, you don't want to leave." ■

Two days from port in Adelaide, the 22.8m fishing vessel *Diana* ploughs through a light Southern Ocean swell, on course for the seamounts of the Great Australian Bight.

Up to 7500 baited hooks, attached to longlines, get shot out and hauled back in each day. Every one of them has to be straightened or replaced before the next run. Brent 'Lakey' Carney is hard at work to make sure the hooks are ready to go.

Heave away, haul away!

Longline fishing crews brave some of southern Australia's wildest waves
for days on end to put blue-eye trevalla and pink ling on our tables.

Issue 107 Mar-Apr 2012

STORY BY **PHIL JARRATT** PHOTOGRAPHY BY **DEAN SAFFRON**

I AM WOKEN SUDDENLY and violently by a massive wave slamming into *Diana*'s bow, sending shudders through the forward hatch, where my bunk allows just enough space to swat a fly or hold a book at reading distance. A thin, steel membrane separates me from the heaving Great Australian Bight, and through it I can hear the roar of exploding waves as I retrieve myself from the bunk's safety net. A front has hit, unleashing 40-knot winds and huge swells on this small boat on a big sea.

Above the din I can hear the chant of the skipper, Russell 'Harry' Potter: "Buoy please…weight mate…buoy thanks." I flick on the dim overhead light and check my watch. It's 1am and out on the gale-whipped deck, Harry and his crew are 'shooting out' – feeding 2.1km-long lines into the depths, each carrying 1500 baited hooks.

Front or no front, it's business as usual on the longliner *Diana*. If skipper and crew want to hit port with money in their pockets, they must ignore the driving rain, wind and salt spray in order to bait hooks, feed line and haul weights in the icy darkness for one last time on this 10-day trip.

I can picture the scene without leaving my bunk. The skipper is in the wheelhouse following the 3-D modelling of the ocean bottom on a computer screen, spacing floats and weights according to the seamount contours more than 500m below us. "Buoy thanks…now a weight…" It is intense, mind-numbing work. But at least he is dry and has something to hold on to. Another wave slams the boat. Out on the work deck I can hear David 'River' Carlson – the oldest, gnarliest, toughest and most artfully tattooed of the deckhands – cursing and cackling like a maniac. We're being pitched like a cork and 'Old Man River' is out in the bitter darkness, loving every minute.

Photographer Dean Saffron and I joined *Diana* at Dock 2, Port Adelaide, and greeted the crew. Harry, 41, is cleancut, fit-looking with a quiet manner and ready smile. Kyle 'Inchy' Brown, 23, is the baby-faced first mate; young to have such responsibility but, says his skipper, destined to one day take the helm. At 43, River is the old man of the boat: a tough-looking customer whose crooked smile is equally frightening and reassuring. Ash Rayner, 31, is a bodyboarding lady-killer whose family grew grapes in McLaren Vale, SA. Brent 'Lakey' Carney, 20, is a third-generation fisherman who's been on boats since he was a toddler. River volunteers the story behind Lakey's nickname: "When he first come on the boat he followed me around everywhere and I'd keep running into him. River runs into a lake, get it? He's still bloody doing it!"

Demersal auto longlining – the type of fishing done from *Diana* – often gets bad press due to confusion with pelagic longlining. Demersal longlining is bottom fishing and can target specific species. The bycatch – mostly sharks – can be set free while still alive. Pelagic longliners, which hunt tuna, haul tens of thousands of hooks along the surface and are criticised for snaring seabirds, dolphins and seals along with their catch.

Will Mure, chief executive of Mures, the Hobart-based seafood wholesaler and retailer that owns *Diana*, says all forms of fishing have their critics. "For the restaurant we buy from all types of fishing operations," he explains, "so it would be hypocritical of me to stand in judgement."

Will's dad, George Mure, and his skipper Martin Beck began dropline fishing in Bass Strait in 1977. By the 1990s Will was running the fishing operation and in 1995 he took on Harry, a young short-order cook keen to give fishing a go, who threw up for most of his first day and on into the night. $\longrightarrow$

"You'll be right when the Sun comes up," Will told him.

Harry persevered and within a couple of years had his skipper's ticket and was running the boat, but it was not big enough for longer trips, so Mure commissioned the purpose-built 22.8m *Diana*, which was delivered early in 2004 at a cost of $2.5 million [2012 values]. Will shared the wheelhouse with his protégé for the first few days before handing the boat over to Harry, who has been at the helm since, taking *Diana* from the high seas off Australia's east coast to the Arafura Sea and to the seamounts of the Great Australian Bight.

There are rewards, Harry says, but it isn't an easy life. As we steam into the night down the long fetch of the Gulf St Vincent, the roll of the boat becomes more pronounced. Headed for the Southern Ocean, we know to expect more of this.

By morning we are in a real sea and I'm as sick as a dog. With another 18 hours of steaming to reach the seamounts, I just have to tough it out. I've been out in small boats plenty of times, but I'm not handling this vessel's pitch and diesel smell. The skipper offers to fix me a feed. I'm halfway through a bacon-and-egg sandwich when for the first, but not the last, time I make a hasty exit. When I return Harry says: "You'll be right when the Sun comes up."

We motor towards the mounts for another six hours and then everyone is hustled out of bed to start work at 1am. It takes several hours as up to five magazines are fed out, each one with 2100m of monofilament line and 1500 hooks spaced 1.4m apart and baited with mackerel. When the lines are set, the skipper sets a course to idle back in the direction of the first line, then it's back to bed to catch a couple more hours sleep.

At 7am the hand on watch wakes the rest of the crew and the day's real work starts – the hauling in. There's barely time for an instant coffee, let alone breakfast, and the best the crew can hope for – until a 15-minute lunch break after the third line – is a dash to the galley for toast or a muesli bar.

There are only six demersal auto longliners licensed to operate in Australian waters, but our first day's fishing is complicated by the fact that one of them has set its lines across the same seamount and two have crossed. Harry reaches the other skipper by satellite phone while the crew attempts to undo the tangle. Each magazine is worth $3500, and as captain and crew get paid on profit share, it's a bread-and-butter issue.

Dean and I volunteer to cook dinner; him meatballs in sauce, me mashed potatoes. I cut up three times more spuds than I think are necessary and throw them into a huge pot. But the skipper replaces it with a bigger pot and throws another dozen spuds on the bench for me to prepare. It's ordinary fare, but the ravenous crew devour it in minutes.

I sleep in snatches as the men work through the blow. I understand why Harry has them out there – during six days of fishing we'd only averaged a little over a tonne a day – and this is his last chance to boost the catch. But these conditions are close to unworkable. Another wave slams us sideways, and I close my eyes again.

At 7am I hear the skipper on the intercom, but it isn't the enthusiastic cheer with which he greets the start of most hauls. I realise something is seriously wrong. Harry looks tired and forlorn. He bites his lip and curses to himself. The lines have drifted. This last attempt to make the numbers look better could turn out to be an expensive disaster.

I'm beginning to understand the lot of the longline fisherman. For more than a week, Harry has been a mate to us landlubbers, always affable, always in quiet control of his boat. But when it comes down to it, he alone is in charge of seven lives and $3 million worth of equipment, under dangerous conditions.

By midday we have recovered three of five lines with minimal damage, although one had drifted more than 2 nautical miles across a jagged ocean floor. As the last line is hauled in, we've also managed a half-tonne catch. We begin the 28-hour steam for Port Adelaide and the skipper allows himself a wry smile. "Lost the plot a bit there today," Harry says. "Sorry about that."

Diana slams through the swells and somewhere down below River is roaring with laughter and slagging the hapless Lakey. It's business as usual and we're heading for port. ∎

The roads less travelled

Life in the remote Cape York community of
Portland Roads is determined by the natural rhythms
of ocean and weather.

Issue 56 Oct-Dec 1999

STORY AND PHOTOGRAPHY BY **TIM ELLIOTT**

THE SPANISH MACKEREL came out of the water thrashing madly, its sequined flank flashing in the sunshine. With a smooth toss, Greg 'Westy' Westcott reefed the 25kg fish up and over the side of his tiny boat, which at just 8m didn't seem much bigger than the fish. He tried slinging it straight into the kill bin – where fish are slaughtered – but it barely fitted. Finally, after wrestling it into the bin, Westy stood back, hands on hips, his shock of sandy hair waving in the breeze. "Now that is a beautiful creature," he bellowed.

A resident of nearby Portland Roads, a tiny Cape York Peninsula community 500km north of Cairns, Westy fishes for a living. The waters here offer a stunning variety of fish – from coral trout to barramundi to massive dome-headed Maori wrasse – but Westy's a 'macky man' through and through.

"It's a bloody art," he enthused, explaining that he hadn't known much about catching fish when he came here from Brisbane six years ago. "You have to be a mechanic, a navigator, an electrician and a weatherman. Then you have to understand the mackerel itself; where he'll be, what he's thinkin'…when it all comes together, it's magic."

The 'Roads' began as a Depression-era gold mining settlement and was then a World War II Royal Australian Air Force outpost. Like most residents now, Westy's life is ruled by tides, currents and the weather. I'd caught two flights, driven three hours on rutted dirt tracks up to the Portland Roads dead-end and sweated litres in the blood-temperature air to find this tropical hamlet of barely 50 souls set into a jungled hill overlooking the Coral Sea.

Westy's skin is leathery and the same rusty ochre colour as the earth that lines the roads here. He's wiry too; his arms long and toned from hauling in up to 50 big mackerel a day, which he guts, fillets and sends to Cairns where his agent sells it.

"Remoteness is a big part of the Roads, which brings out the best – and worst – in people," he said. "I've now spent two Wets in a row up here, which is usually the time most locals get out."

As respite from city living, it doesn't get much better than Portland Roads. There are no pubs, no clubs and few cars. The main road is a narrow track skirting the palm-fringed beach, with brumbies grazing beneath the trees. Even the houses – open-sided Queenslanders – are hard to spot, sitting snugly in the lap of a thickly forested hill.

During the 1920s, Kuuku-ya'u clan Aboriginals were forcibly moved to nearby missions like Lockhart River, 20km to the south, but their descendants maintain close ties to traditional lands here. Black, white; young, old; everyone shares that odd, filial warmth peculiar to small communities – an underlying mistrust of outsiders and undeclared respect nourished by common experience.

For almost two decades, Arthur 'Chips' Chippendale and wife Pam have shared those experiences. I met them at their Chili Beach home, about 6km south of Portland Roads. "Why did we come up here?" Chips mused, leaning into his seat and cracking a drink. "Guess we just got sick of the life we were leading in Brisbane… I thought there had to be a better way."

Better it might be, but easier it wasn't. After a couple of years as caretakers on Restoration Island, 1km off the coast, Chips and Pam moved to their current idyllic plot backing onto a pocket-sized private bay. Along with chooks, their property supports limes, pawpaws, bananas, avocados, custard apples and an old mango tree that towers over the yard like a giant green storm cloud.

While Chips fished, Pam established a taxi run, which she operated until recently, covering the two-hour trip south to

Tropical clouds filter the late afternoon sun as prawners prepare for another night at sea. Living with nature and tough as nails, the fishers are emblematic of the Roads.

Lockhart River, an Aboriginal settlement of 500 with basic amenities. The road between it and Portland Roads often floods in the Wet, meaning the Chippendales can be cut off for months at a time.

A barge with over-priced, yellowing vegetables arrives from Cairns fortnightly, except when it stops in the Wet. So Pam and Chips have learnt to be self-sufficient. They have a 1.5 tonne fridge that, when fully stocked with meat and vegetables, and supplemented with fresh fish, can see them through at least four months. Electricity comes from generators. And, being a long way from mains supply, they catch water in rainwater tanks.

I was dropped off at the mouth of the Pascoe River, 20km north-west of Portland Roads, and hitched a ride to Wattle Hills, 15km upriver, in a dinghy with resident Kenny Whitehead, to meet with Frenchwoman Stephanie Thuillier, who ran the Eclectus Wilderness Retreat birdwatchers' lodge.

When we arrived, Stephanie was wielding a mattock on a patch of scrub, sweat flying off her like liquid sparks. She welcomed us in a heavy Parisian brogue, shaking my hand so hard I thought it would come off my wrist. Taking us inside for a drink, she reeled off a list of the area's impressive birdlife: the palm cockatoo, yellow-billed kingfisher, magnificent riflebird, southern cassowary and fawn-breasted bowerbird.

Stephanie arrived here in '84 on holidays with then-partner Kim and they decided to stay. By working as cooks on board ships and trawlers they raised enough money to start two restaurants, including one in the Roads. When land in Wattle Hills became available they pounced, moving in during the 1992 dry season and building with whatever was at hand. After six years and two floods, Kim left.

Back at the Roads I drop in on "real long-time local" Geoff Pope. As the local postie he has "the closest thing to an official position anybody's got round here". Like most of his fellow residents he was aloof yet engaging, with a wit so dry it rattled.

"To people living in the city a remote lifestyle sounds good," he says of Portland Roads. "But when they actually try it they can't hack it… The people who survive up here are the people who can adapt. The most important thing is to let people be what they want to be. And don't tread on any toes. It's all about respect: not much to ask, really." ■

Island fantasy

The Whitsundays' lesser known neighbours, the
South Cumberland Islands, are nine low peaks set
adrift upon the Coral Sea.

Issue 128 Sep-Oct 2015

STORY BY **ASHLEY HAY** PHOTOGRAPHY BY **ANDREW GREGORY**

WE WERE CROSSING the hillside when we saw a koala tucked into a wild prune tree, a metre or so above us. It was late March and a southerly wind dulled the still-harsh autumnal sun on St Bees, an 1100ha island, 30km north-east of Mackay, on the Queensland coast.

We had bush-bashed through a particular sort of Australian landscape to find these docile marsupials: eucalypts and figs mixed with prickly pear and lantana. Looking down from the koala's hill, we were greeted by a fairytale picture of soft green grasses and dark green hoop pines.

St Bees is bordered by the 650m-wide Egremont Passage, a deep blue expanse, beyond which the sculptured velveteen shapes of Keswick Island rise from the sea like a nest of slumbering prehistoric creatures. Keswick and St Bees are among nine islands lying south of the better-known Whitsundays and protected within South Cumberland Islands National Park.

Adding to the fairytale aura, the air was thick with butterflies. More than 40 species, including the ubiquitous blue tiger, have been recorded across these islands. There are also shorebirds, curlews, bats, owls and whales. And there are reefs – a trip in a glass-bottomed boat reveals vast staghorn forests, brilliant iridescent corals and myriad fishes. "You see everything here," says Brett Curd, Keswick Island's operations officer. "We've had black-tipped and white-tipped reef sharks, leopard rays, dolphins and even manta rays...there's a turtle," he adds as one goes by, its head bobbing out of the water. Employed by Keswick Developments, it's Brett's job to oversee everything from construction and landscaping to running the local shop and the island's runway: "I'm the council, the mayor, the labour and the manager."

We'd come to the islands in the off-season, at the tail end of cyclone time. Temperatures peaked around 30°C by day and the water wasn't much cooler at about 26°C.

These islands are far more than coconut-palm-fringed getaways. In biogeographic terms, St Bees and Keswick have been fantastic field laboratories for exploring how resident species interact with each other and with flora and fauna on neighbouring islands.

The koalas are one example. They were relocated from Proserpine, 125km north of Mackay, in the 1930s. But while island populations tend to thrive or fail, these animals have maintained a stable colony. To scientists, this is a conundrum.

The puzzle first attracted attention in the late 1990s and remains unexplained, says Dr Alistair Melzer, a Central Queensland University ecologist. The bacterial disease chlamydia ravages many other koala populations, causing high rates of infertility, but although it's been detected in a few St Bees' koalas, it doesn't seem to be impacting numbers. And although most adult females give birth each year, the population doesn't increase.

"Something happens to the joeys around the point of weaning, and a lot of them just disappear," Alistair explains. "They're too small to tag, so we've got no way of tracking them...[they] seem to be absolutely fine one day and gone the next."

Another investigation, funded by conservation body Earthwatch, is based on what Alistair calls 'big biome shifts' that are taking place on islands like these: grasslands being replaced by woodlands; woodlands being replaced by rainforests. There are climate shifts occurring, Alistair says, and there are also changes to historical grazing and fire regimes. Using altitudinal plots, weather sensors and historical data, he hopes that St Bees will become the case study for understanding island ecosystem changes for the entire region.

Tropical islands have long fed fantasies, and Keswick has a smattering of permanent residents who are living that dream. Among them are Ron and Marion Brooks, who settled per-

The South Cumberland group's main islands Keswick (top right) and St Bees are separated by the Egremont Passage, a 25m-deep crossing created by a drowned valley.

manently in 2008. The island is just 530ha and only 20 or so houses line its streets. Seasonal visitors arrive from Easter and leave in November and in the off-season, Keswick's population comprises about a dozen people.

A more abundant population of another kind exists on the island's northern side. Looking a lot like a collection of letterboxes or filing cabinets sits an installation of miscellaneous containers. They're beehives, the first of which were brought to Keswick from Innisfail in 1985. They were – and still are – free from any major diseases. So while diseases such as chalkbrood (which appeared in Queensland in 1993) and the varroa mite (which hasn't reached Australia) ravage hives and colonies around the world, queens from Keswick have been posted across Australia and beyond to ensure the propagation of healthy new generations.

It's not an enormous trade – just short of two dozen clean queens have left Keswick in the last two years – but it's an important one. The queens can't remedy existing diseases, but they introduce infection-free generations of pollinators. And the honey made here is spectacular. Flavoured by nectar from the local grass trees and other distinct blooms, it has a deep, dark-red colour and tastes like malted caramel.

Keswick has plentiful gardens for its tiny residents, well-tended pockets against the lush green natural bush. The island's development lease was granted more than eight years ago and Brett Curd became its operations officer. The plan was to regenerate its community spaces with plants imported from the mainland.

"Then we discovered we had our own horticulturalists," says Brett, referring to Ron and Marion Brooks, who took on running the nursery. Seeds from the island were collected and propagated, and the nursery now holds Keswick's flora in miniature: from native ginger and beach cherry to cotton trees and grass trees.

Perhaps it's the kind of self-sufficiency islands foster. Keswick has no natural springs; rather, rain fills the tanks that supply its water. Power is solar, and wastes, including black water, are processed on-site, with only the hardest rubbish shipped back to the mainland.

"It makes me laugh when people talk about this 'new' ecotourism and sustainability," Brett says. "We've been doing it here for years." ∎

The granite cliffs of White Water Wall are a favourite with experienced rock climbers like Bob McMahon, pictured at left.

Beyond the bay

Look past the obvious curve of Wineglass Bay and you'll discover other remarkable treasures on the Freycinet Peninsula.

Issue 109 Jul-Sep 2012

STORY BY **ANDREW BAIN**
PHOTOGRAPHY BY **NICK RAINS**

O N THE EAST COAST of Tasmania's Freycinet Peninsula, the Tasman Sea is surging, showering the granite cliffs of White Water Wall. Bob McMahon dips a hand in his chalk bag, and a puff of powder disappears into the spray. He begins to climb, his hands and feet drawn to holds by years of familiarity.

It's 33 years since Bob made the first climb on 'Beowulf', a route that traverses above a sea cave, on rock scratched and notched by time and tide. It was an era when he had a virtual monopoly on new climbing routes at Freycinet, including the peninsula's first recorded climb in 1969 on Sow Spur. "It was always about new routes, first ascents, discovering places," he says. "One weekend…I think we did 32 new routes in a bit over a day."

Look around Freycinet National Park and you could be forgiven for thinking he needn't have hurried. Although Freycinet is one of Tasmania's most popular national parks – visited by more than 200,000 people a year – few visitors see beyond the perfect curve of Wineglass Bay, a beach that's over-shadowed everything else here ever since colonial times. "The view was like enchantment," author and artist Louisa Meredith wrote after visiting in 1853. "Far below my giddy perch…lay, calmly slumbering in the bright sunshine, the blue and beautiful nook of the Pacific named Wineglass Bay."

For ranger-in-charge Rob Connell, it's a familiar refrain. "Really, the park starts and ends for maybe 80 per cent of people at the [Wineglass Bay] lookout," he says. "But for the 20 per cent who want to go further, that's where the fun begins." $\longrightarrow$

On a map Freycinet Peninsula comes close to being a place set apart from Tasmania, hanging off its east coast like the chain of islands Abel Tasman mistook it for in 1642. It seems somehow fitting, because Freycinet's history is also far removed from the typical Tasmanian tale of convict influence.

Tin, coal and granite have all been mined on the peninsula and its islands. Sealers worked its shores in the early 19th century, followed in 1824 by the first whaling station on Tasmania's east coast. Up to nine whaling stations operated on the peninsula, and on Schouten and Refuge islands, including a station at the southern end at Wineglass Bay, which at times ran foul with blood.

"When we'd pull the boat up at the southern end of Wineglass, you could still see whale bones down through the water," says local artist Vanessa Quilliam. "There's so much history here, it's crazy. Freycinet went from being such a hive of industry and activity, straight to being a national park, and everything was just left and not preserved."

Finding material evidence of the early activity isn't easy, though traces do exist. A granite quarry scars the base of Mt Mayson. Farmhouses stand behind Moreys Bay (Schouten Island) and Cooks Beach as reminders of early sheep and cattle grazing.

Even among the relics, however, it's clear that, almost 100 years since the creation of the national park, nature has fought its way back into the ascendancy. On Schouten Island little penguins shuffle past the remains of whaling tryworks each night. White-bellied sea eagles command nests as large as rafts, and the largest visitors of all, southern right and humpback whales, are back in force.

When the French explorer Nicolas Baudin sailed along Tasmania's east coast 160 years after Tasman, he corrected the Dutchman's mapping error, recognising Freycinet as a peninsula and naming it for the brothers Louis and Henri Freycinet. He also named Fleurieu Bay, a body of water so rich with native angasi oysters it was later renamed Great Oyster Bay. Today, it continues to produce oysters in abundance, and oyster farms are the only significant primary industry.

Giles Fisher is owner of Freycinet Marine Farm, and one of six oyster-licence holders on the peninsula. "Oyster Bay fattens oysters beautifully. It's like a factory. You never have to worry about environmental conditions; it just does it. It's got a very strong circular current flow and water just races past, creating a really lovely food delivery system."

I've joined Giles on his punt, *Perseverance*, skimming across the Swan River estuary with a stacked load of oyster baskets.

Giles steps down into the waist-deep water and begins walking upstream, clipping baskets on to lines. It's been his routine since he and wife Julia bought Freycinet Marine Farm seven years ago, after almost a decade working in the salmon industry on Tasmania's west coast.

"We genuinely have people clamouring for our oysters," Giles says. "They seem to have a nice sweet flavour that people find very enjoyable. That's not our doing – I'd love to take credit for it – it's the water, and it's the area we're in."

In the past seven years, Giles has boosted oyster stocks from 90,000 to about 4.6 million. Three years ago he opened a farm-gate stall – a tin shed in a paddock – that has become Freycinet's busiest eatery, feeding up to 500 people a day in summer. But Giles and Julia didn't move to Freycinet for business. "We moved here because it was a really lovely place to be," Giles says. "We decided we wanted to live here and then we were lucky enough to find the industry that matched what I'd been doing. I'll finish work and go for a swim on the beach, and you've got four to choose from. I wouldn't move now for a million bucks."

Look at the raw infrastructure of Coles Bay, and it could be any small country town: one pub, a post office, one restaurant, no school. No road reached the town until the 1920s, and it wasn't sealed for another 60 years. Electricity didn't arrive until 1963. Yet Coles Bay sits at the doorstep of Wineglass Bay, one of the most instantly recognisable natural features in Australia.

Although tourism has been Coles Bay's mainstay since Harry Parsons built the first shacks at The Fisheries in the 1920s, the town retains an understated atmosphere. Only about 150–200 people live here permanently, surrounded by

The pink granite of The Hazards (opposite) dominates the skyline on Freycinet Peninsula's southern end.

Large numbers of 400-million-year-old marine fossils (left) were uncovered by bushfires that ripped through the Friendly Beaches area towards the northern end of Freycinet NP in 2005.

weekend holiday homes. Out in the bay a mere handful of yachts roll about calmly, sheltered from any wind except a south-westerly.

"When I was a kid, all this bay was lit up right across there with scallop boats," says born-and-bred Coles Bay resident Grant Whelan. "There was a little jetty and it'd be nothing to see 30 or 40 boats tied up here."

At 62, Grant has been fishing from Coles Bay for 46 years. For about the past 20 years, his crayboat *Southern Cross* has been the town's only commercial fishing vessel.

Time, though, has brought minimal change to Coles Bay itself. In recent years Coles Bay residents and shack owners have resisted the construction of a marina, a large supermarket and a second caravan park. When Alex and Rosie Kain, owners of Iluka Holiday Centre, wanted to build the town's pub, it became a four-year fight all the way to the Supreme Court. It's blunted none of their enthusiasm for the place.

"It's lovely to live here," says Alex. "Rosie's been here since 1966 on and off, and I started coming here in '77. Other than the roads being sealed and the number of people coming through, not much has changed in that time. I reckon it will always stay that way."

On the slopes of The Hazards, beside the famed Wineglass Bay Lookout, Rob Connell admires what so few people see from here. "If you stop and take your time to look at the rocks, some of them will take your breath away," he says. "You'll see this enormous rock the size of a house balanced on one tiny point. I never get sick of looking at that."

For this geologist-turned-ranger, Freycinet is a dream posting. From across Coles Bay, the bare 370-million-year-old granite of The Hazards glows in almost pinkish tones created by the feld-spar within the rock. Head a short distance south and a distinct fault line cuts through the western edge of the peninsula and across the middle of Schouten Island.

"What we see today are these really distinctive landscapes formed by the juxtaposition of these two rock types – the gran-ite, which is quite bare and eroded with very few trees; and the dolerite soils, which are much more fertile and have heathlands and eucalypts," Rob says.

As we continue walking, threading between granite boulders, we come to the lookout platform, which hangs off the slopes of Mt Amos. Every year about 100,000 people climb to this spot to marvel at the symmetry of the beach below. Yet as I look around at Freycinet's mountains, bush and ocean, it's clear that even from here, Wineglass Bay is only a small part of the view. ∎

The incessant wind etches patterns in the sand along the beach on Younghusband Peninsula, Coorong National Park, South Australia.

Close encounters of the bird kind

Wild, windswept Coorong National Park is a nature lover's paradise.

Issue 36 Oct-Dec 1994

TEXT BY **JENNY STANTON**
PHOTOGRAPHY BY **MIKE LANGFORD**

PELICANS HOVERED overhead, bobbed on the choppy waters around me and huddled in huge groups on a windswept hillside some 100m away. I was on North Pelican Island in the heart of South Australia's Coorong National Park, surrounded by thousands of these large black-and-white birds with long pouched bills, but my eyes were drawn to four downy chicks just 20m ahead.

Stumbling about clumsily through stinging nettles on pink feet, it was hard to believe that in two or three months these gawky chicks would be transformed into magnificent flying machines. My guide David Dadd, who has supervised a banding program for the past five years as part of a CSIRO study of pelican movements, estimated that they were about 30 days old. They'd have left the nest just days previously to join a creche, where they'd remain for two or three months until fully fledged.

I'd joined David and his wife Margaret on their annual recce of the island. With at least 5000 pelicans, it supports what is believed to be Australia's largest permanent breeding colony. Banders are allowed limited access but anyone else who strays within 140m faces stiff penalties.

We clambered from our boat and over the jagged limestone fringing the tiny island. Most of the adult pelicans were away feeding or had flown off as we approached. David and Margaret stopped frequently to note positions and relative sizes of chicks, estimating they'd be able to be banded within a couple of weeks. It's indicative of the Coorong site's significance to Australian pelicans that bands have been recovered in all mainland States except Western Australia, and from as far north as Papua New Guinea. $\longrightarrow$

I'd had my first glimpse from a pelican's perspective of the 46,745ha Coorong National Park a week earlier, flying with pilot Neville Grills and district ranger Phil Hollow. Bordered by the Southern Ocean to the west and Princes Highway to the east, the park – which was immortalised in Colin Thiele's classic children's book *Storm Boy* – is no more than 5km wide but stretches 140km south-east from the Murray Mouth, where the Murray River reaches the sea. Recognised internationally as a major waterfowl and migratory bird refuge, more than half is covered by water. Access is possible only via 4WD tracks or boat.

"People don't realise the amount of water until they see it from the air," Neville commented as we flew south-east down the 100km length of the Coorong, the narrow saltwater lagoon after which the park is named. Where the water petered out into a series of salt lakes, we turned and headed north-west, over the sand dunes of the narrow Younghusband Peninsula, which separates the Coorong from the sea.

Retired ranger and keen birdwatcher Herman Bakker later took me to the peninsula to show me his favourite spot in the park. Herman, his wife Colleen and I rose at sunrise, once the winds that whip the lagoon into a mass of whitecaps for much of the spring and early summer had eased, and paddled the 2.5km from Noonameena to Younghusband Peninsula.

There we beached our canoes on pristine wind-rippled sand and hiked to a dune overlooking the beach, from where I could just make out the outline of Kangaroo Island 100km to our west. Herman pointed out two black-and-white birds dodging the surf – endangered hooded plovers, one of the park's 238 bird species. These threatened plovers nest on the sand and their dwindling numbers have led to vehicles being banned from part of the beach at the height of the nesting season.

As well as being a waterbird haven of international signif-icance, the Coorong is an important archaeological site. Its eastern shore would have been covered by mallee scrub in 1830, when Charles Sturt became the first European to explore the lower Murray.

Today, due to agricultural clearing, it's a different story. "This is the only decent bit of native vegetation left," explained Tom Trevorrow, as we stood on 800ha Bonney Reserve, near Noon-ameena.

The reserve is in the care of Camp Coorong, an Aboriginal cultural centre where Tom and other Ngarrindjeri people work. Educational groups can stay at the camp and learn first-hand about the Ngarrindjeris' long association with the Coorong, which stretches back well over 5000 years.

Commercial fishers also have an intense interest in the Coorong. Garry Hera-Singh is a third-generation fisherman but representative of a new breed anxious to improve the Coorong's long-term fishing potential. He's one of 38 fishermen in the Coorong fishery. Their annual catch is worth as much as $2.5 million [1994 values] and supports up to 80 families.

The Coorong's water comes from the Southern Ocean and Murray River and, to a lesser extent, rainfall and groundwater. In 1935 – following pressure from farmers – work began on 7.6km of barrages to stop saltwater entering the lower Murray via lakes Albert and Alexandrina. They were completed in 1940 and have more than halved the flow from the Murray into the Coorong. It's resulted in the northern Coorong becoming more saline and less freshwater available to scour a channel at the Murray Mouth.

The southern lagoon – south of Parnka Point – is affected by more complex factors because it receives little freshwater from the Murray. Lack of freshwater, coupled with high evaporation rates, means salinity levels there can be three to five times that of normal seawater. Fishermen such as Garry have been lobbying to have more freshwater channelled in to decrease salinity and increase fish habitat.

I spent my final morning at Pelican Point, watching the sun's first rays light up the dunes of Younghusband Peninsula. Pelicans eyed me from roosts on wooden poles and black swans glided gracefully by. It was the archetypal Coorong scene and I was reminded of a passage from Colin Thiele's book: "No-one can live out a week's quiet days by the Coorong's seascape, sandscape or fronded shore without some kind of spiritual rebirth." ∎

Garry Hera-Singh and Bill Selby display two of the 10 mulloway that made up the previous evening's 150kg haul. Most of the fish, weighing up to 20kg a piece, are sold in markets. Garry and Bill are two of the 28 fisherman in the Coorong fishery. "It's one of the major employers in the area, along with agriculture and tourism," he says.

David and Margaret Dadd (opposite), who supervise a bird banding program, inspect a pelican nest on an island rookery in the heart of Coorong National Park.

A town like Dongara

How the rock lobster converted a humble WA fishing
village into a community of millionaires.

Issue 75 Jul-Sep 2004

STORY BY **ANDREW PERRIN** PHOTOGRAPHY BY **THOMAS WIELECKI**

THE WESTERN ROCK lobster or crayfish is the reason the small west coast hamlets of Dongara and Port Denison have perhaps more millionaires per capita than any other place in Australia. This non-descript bit of coast – with 3000 residents, three churches, two pubs and one drive-in – annually injects more than $50 million [2004 values] into the Australian economy.

Dongara used to be little more than a fuel stop between Perth and Geraldton. But when Perth entrepreneur Theo Kailis began selling live lobsters to Asia in 1992, Dongara's fisher-men found themselves sitting on a goldmine. Soon, the price of a lobster licence doubled, trebled, then quadrupled. Now a licence can't be bought for less than $2 million. State-of-the-art fishing boats, like those tied up at Dongara's marina, begin at $500,000. But money hasn't changed the town's essential character.

Though many here can afford to take four months off a year, fishermen still get around in shorts and singlets. Meanwhile, the town enjoys one of Australia's lowest crime rates. "People here don't need to steal," says police sergeant Mark Bushell.

Peter 'Kakka' Hope, retired lobster fisherman and now a volunteer golf-course greenkeeper, likes to remember the way it was before GPS and computerised depth sounders were used to identify the most fertile fishing ground. In the 1950s, Peter and his dad even used empty bottles as floats. "Great days," he says, then adds with a smile, "but these are better."

"All this good fortune wouldn't be worth a cracker if it'd corrupted people's souls," says Benedictine monk Reverend Dom Justin Bruce. "But the real miracle of Dongara is this: it hasn't."

This was once a town divided. On one side of the Irwin River was Dongara, a meeting place and retirement vil-lage for farmers in moleskins and tweed jackets. On the other

was Port Denison where the fishermen – barefoot and in shorts – lived with their raucous families in fibro shacks.

The class barrier didn't sit well with a young John Cole, a farmer's son who spent much of his youth in the 1950s on a boat his father bought him to earn a little extra money. "It always seemed to me that fishermen were downtrodden, looked down upon, and I always felt that was a shame," John says. "So I felt if there was something I could do to help make a better livelihood for fishermen, I'd do it." John spent 26 years as president of the WA Fishing Industry Council, deftly navigating the industry through its transformation from irrelevance to one of Australia's largest export earners. But John never failed to return to Dongara and his boat. "It's a great life," he says. "And there's no shame in being a fisherman anymore."

Peter Hope's mother, Sheila Hope, used to hang her red dressing-gown on the washing line to warn her husband the fishing inspector was in town. "We'd have to dump all the kakkas [undersized lobsters] over the side," Peter says. In 1972 he bought his own licence for $7000 and, when the industry boomed, promptly got out – flush with cash. Others in town were not so lucky. Deckhand Gary 'Bo' Bovell applied to buy a fishing licence in the 1970s but his bank manager rejected his loan application. "To this day I'd like to wring that bank manager's neck," he says.

Irrespective of how well anyone's travelling, Dongara retains social cohesion, with practically the whole town turning up at the drive-in on a Friday night.

Don't expect to find BMWs in the driveways of million dollar homes overlooking the beach. "People here are wealthy yet money is not their obsession," says farmer and shire coun-cillor Lynton Watson. "It's simply allowed people to do what they always did, except now they can do it a bit better."

As dawn breaks, deckhand Michael Farmer has already been at work for two hours hauling up crammed lobster pots from the sea floor.

Most of Dongara's fishermen got their start in the industry working as deckhands. "In the old days you could work on the back of a boat for a few years, save a few bob, and buy yourself a licence," says fisherman Peter Campbell.

Not anymore. The cost of licences today is prohibitive. Michael Butcher, 19, is the son of a fisherman and hopes to get his dad's boat when he retires. Veteran deckie Doug Bowen missed his opportunity to buy a licence when he first began working on deck in the 1970s, yet, despite a dodgy elbow, knees and back, and seawater boils that won't heal, he has no regrets: "I still enjoy the sight of hauling up a pot filled with crayfish." The sight thrills professionals and amateurs alike. Most of Dongara's regular citizens don't miss the chance to "pull their pots" – amateurs are restricted to two – from the bottom of the harbour each morning.

Dongara's CEO, John Merrick, and Mark Luzi, the town planner, start their day at the harbour, alongside the town's school principal, bank manager, police sergeant, gardener and publican. "It's like panning for gold," John says. "Only you can't eat gold."

It's the end of a hard day for Doug Bowen aboard the lobster boat *Wave Cruiser*. But for the 140kg of lobster he and his boss Peter Campbell deliver to the M.G. Kailis processing factory in Port Denison harbour, it's the beginning of a remarkable journey. Packers like Beryl Sing sift through the day's catch, selecting the hardiest specimens for the long flight to Asia. Once chosen, the lobsters are put in cold water, slowing their metabolic rate. Packed tight inside a polystyrene box and covered with woodchips, it appears unlikely these seemingly delicate animals could survive the journey. But they do.

Within 23 hours of being packed they land in Asia, ready for delivery to the many restaurants specialising in fresh seafood. Despite Asia's insatiable appetite for this Australian delicacy, the supply won't dry up. As one of the world's first managed fisheries, the western rock-lobster fishery has been studied since the early 1960s. This enables scientists to accurately predict catches and fishery managers to ensure controls are adequate to protect breeding stocks.

"The situation we have here is the envy of the world," says Fisheries WA scientist Nick Caputi. If Australia is the lucky country, Dongara may well be its luckiest town. ∎

Surfers like Michael Harvey often use the Cape to Cape Track to access the coastline's many famous surf breaks.

Cape of contrast

WA's Cape to Cape Track was forged from sheer determination – and thousands of hikers reap the benefits each year.

Issue 98 Apr-Jun 2010

STORY BY **JAMES MCCORMACK**
PHOTOGRAPHY BY **ANDREW GREGORY**

THE WHALES ARE breaching in unison. Minutes earlier, five humpbacks were launching up out of the water at once. Now, in perfect symmetry, two are arcing high into the air, like synchronised swimmers or trained dolphins, with not a fin out of place. Even Bill Webb – a Wardandi elder who has been fishing here since childhood and has seen thousands of breaches – is shouting in excitement.

Bill and fellow Wardandi man Josh Whiteland have taken me along a track, well-defined at first but then a scramble, to one of their favourite rock-fishing spots. They were fired up to get down here, and with good reason: it's gorgeous. A seal pokes its head from the placid water. Rainbows appear to sprout from the sea as sunlight strikes scattered cloudbursts to the east. Behind us, sea caves drip with so many stalactites it's as if the caves themselves are melting into the ocean. And the whales are breaching, silhouetted against a sky turned saffron by the setting sun. Maps show this place as Cape Naturaliste, but the Wardandi call it Kwirreejeenungup: "the place with the beautiful view".

This is the northern end of WA's Cape to Cape Track, in 19,092ha Leeuwin-Naturaliste National Park. The 135km track – a succession of spectacular headlands, high cliff tops, tall karri forests and long, lonely beaches – runs between Cape Naturaliste and Cape Leeuwin along Australia's most south-westerly coastline. It delivers fishermen such as Bill and Josh to tried-and-tested sites, surfers to challenging and world-famous waves, cavers to exquisite formations and climbers to spectacular granite sea cliffs. There are, of course, also those who come simply to walk the wild stretch of $\longrightarrow$

coast – to trace empty beaches, wend through wind-pruned heath and watch rocks pummelled by swells that have surged unhindered all the way from Africa.

Balance is perhaps the track's defining quality. The obvious point of symmetry is that between sea and land. Water – in turn sparkling and benign, then moody and raging – defines the track's character as much as does the land itself. Beyond this is the balance between beach and forest, comfort and challenge, wilderness and civilisation. Even the geology is balanced: much of the track winds over dunes of limestone less than 2 million years old while the rock beneath – which is exposed at most headlands – is largely ancient granitic gneiss (a type of metamorphic rock) that's 1500–600 million years old.

These contrasts make the track special, says Jane Scott, president of Friends of the Cape to Cape Track. "It's not hugely spectacular with mountain scenery or really high cliffs, but you've got a great variety of landforms and fabulous vegetation. You can really feel totally remote and yet you're only a stone's throw from civilisation."

The track's vegetation gets Jane most excited. Despite having moved here 35 years ago, she's lost neither her clipped English accent nor the thrill of spotting wildflowers. "Ooh!" she cries, as we walk through heath near Redgate Beach. "A donkey orchid! Ooh, ooh, ooh! See that, that lovely flash of blue – *Dampiera linearis!*"

The idea for the Cape to Cape Track began taking shape as early as the 1970s when Jane and her friends would regularly explore this region. In the early 1990s, Jane and caving mate Neil Taylor, Leeuwin–Naturaliste NP's recreation planner, together mapped out a route that linked long sandy beaches, existing and purpose-built walking tracks and old 4WD routes gouged out by farmers, fishermen and surfers. By the late '90s, the national park had commenced the track's construction and in 1998 the Friends group formed to attract grants and funding that the national park couldn't. The track was officially created in 2001.

There are now more than 400 Friends of the track and their small annual subscriptions contribute much needed maintenance funds. Many are retired or semi-retired and also volunteer their time to maintain the track, with about 35 having each 'adopted' a section to care for. Not all track adopters are retired, however. The Margaret River Surfrider Foundation has taken on a 6km section between Ellensbrook and Lefthanders, and 33-year-old Blair Darvill – strong, fit and bronzed – is one of the dozen or so who actively participate.

"It's a pretty famous stretch of coastline. There's at least half a dozen surf breaks along it," says Blair, explaining that the track is the quickest way to access these breaks and surfers have had "quite a bit of impact".

It's an easy start to the track from the north, virtually in the shadow of Cape Naturaliste Lighthouse. The first 3km is hard-surfaced with sections of boardwalk, and winds gently down to Sugarloaf Rock, where red-tailed tropicbirds nest. In spring, there's a riot of wildflowers, their scent so strong that even with an ocean breeze you can't smell the salt air. Conveniently placed benches allow walkers to sit and gaze at the sea or migrating whales, or spy on fluttering wrens. Even south of Sugarloaf Rock, when the path turns to sand, the track maintains its easygoing nature, continuing a gentle descent through wizened heath.

It wanders sedately along limestone cliffs; past fantastically shaped, pockmarked rock; and above coves, beaches and reefs lapped by pale blue water to arrive at The Three Bears (named for its surf breaks: Poppa, Momma and Baby Bear). While these opening sections are pleasant, the track is a lot more challenging than people expect. The proximity to towns and lack of long climbs lead many walkers to underestimate it. There are long sections of calf-burning beach walking – more than 20km in total – and even the formed track is often soft and sandy. It's also the first place in Australia to bear the brunt of gales whipping up off the Southern and Indian oceans.

Jane estimates that 300–400 people walk the track from end to end each year, but many more complete it as a series of day walks. Track access is made easy due to numerous roads run-

At Canal Rocks (left), wave action has carved fractures, faults and bands in softer rocks to create a headland of linear, canal-like channels.

Rottnest tea-trees lining Bunker Bay are contorted by the strong winds that regularly whip up this part of the coastline.

ning down to the coast and the shape of Leeuwin-Naturaliste NP itself. It's a sliver of a reserve, just 120km long and a mere 100m–5km wide, although 21 covenants protecting 450ha of land abutting the park create a sense of greater width.

If you wanted to, you could walk the entire track without coming into contact with civilisation, although that's becoming more difficult. The area has been transformed by the growing popularity of the Margaret River wine region and a local economy boosted by the WA resources boom. Margaret River and Busselton have flourished from increased tourism and subsequent population growth.

In Yallingup, Prevelly and Gracetown, fibro shacks and ramshackle cottages have been replaced by sleek houses and chic cafes and restaurants.

Fifteen years ago, about 900,000 visitors annually came to Leeuwin-Naturaliste NP. Now, about 2.3 million take the trip out to its beaches, forests and caves, making it the most popular national park in WA.

"Managing people is probably the biggest issue we've got," says Glenn Willmott, the park's head ranger. "We've had to put in car parks to protect vegetation. Over the last 15 years, we've probably put in at least 16 toilet blocks, maybe 10 staircases, and six or seven major road improvements. All those things are based on increased visitation."

The further south you head, the wilder the Cape to Cape becomes. Vehicle access becomes increasingly limited. The number of walkers thins. From the high cliffs of Conto the track turns inland, towards the Boranup Forest, where karri trees grow straight and tall. After days of walking on windswept coastline, the contrast is striking. The wind dies, and in the forest's cathedral stillness, birdsong resonates. The Wardandi people talk of a resident devil called Jimidar, who used to sneak around the Boranup menacing women and children and who became incarcerated there until the end of time. Despite the tale, the Boranup is often named by walkers as their favourite section. Perhaps it's because the track here is firm, for the long, wild beach sections aren't far away. "Coming on to Boranup Beach, you've got 8km of soft sand, a pack on your back and a sou'-westerly in your face," says track walker Rob Dickson. "It tests your mettle."

A day's walk further south and you hit a 500m rock platform as holey as Swiss cheese; if the waves, wind and tide are right, blowholes here will rocket water up to 30m into the air. Rounding the headland, you gain your first glimpse of your destination: Cape Leeuwin. There's a remote, pristine, empty beach immediately before you, and in the distance, the tallest lighthouse on the Australian mainland, reminding you that civilisation is not far away. On the Cape to Cape Track, it's all about balance. ∎

In a shimmering sea, Gula Lalara (above) stalks fish as countless generations have done before him. Behind him, his wife Geraldine pulls their outboard runabout, a symbol of the new world that is drawing the Eylandters away from their timeless existence.

Umbakumba teenager Lance Mamarika (right, at right) and his mates Nilton Wanambi and Kevin Mamarika volunteered to carry Ed Stokes's camera bag during an excursion along the island's northern coast. Umbakumba, Groote's second largest community (pop. 300), was established by Fred Gray, a former sea-cucumber fisherman, after Qantas started using nearby Port Langdon as a flying boat base in 1938.

Groote Eylandt – two sides of paradise

A generation after mining came to their island home, Groote Eylandters are meeting the challenge – and paying the price – of their new world.

Issue 24 Oct-Dec 1991

STORY AND PHOTOGRAPHY BY **EDWARD STOKES**

GULA LALARA and Murabuda Wurramarrba braced themselves against our boat's rolls as they scanned the Gulf's wind-lashed water. Groote Eylandt lay astern. "Angry wind," Murabuda shouted, ducking a sheet of spray. Gula and Murabuda were escorting me to Bickerton Island, 20km west of Groote, to introduce me to the smaller island's Aboriginal community. As young men they had often made the crossing – but in dugout canoes, not powerboats.

They had intended to return on the boat later that day, but changed their plans after we landed. "The sea's too rough!" Murabuda exclaimed. "Gula and I been talking. We'll fly back on a charter plane."

I had flown to Groote Eylandt three weeks earlier, passing over Bickerton on the 640km flight from Darwin. My aunt, Judith Stokes, had been sending me occasional letters from Groote since she went to live there more than 30 years earlier, so I knew a bit about it: a 2260sq.km tropical island 50km east of Arnhem Land, home to some 1000 Aborigines, slightly more white Australians – and a manganese mine. But Groote remained mysterious. What was life there really like?

In Angurugu, Judith's home and, with 800 people, Groote's largest Aboriginal community, tamarinds and flame trees provided welcome shade. Stilt houses, some cared for, many tatty, stood in regimented, European order along dusty streets. But the mood was full-blood Aboriginal: bright-eyed kids, shy women in brightly coloured dresses and men gunning 4WDs. At dusk, families gathered around flickering campfires. Voices, music, laughter and heated exchanges drifted through the twilight and blended with the plaintive melodies of amplified gospel singing echoing up from the tamarind grove.

The next morning I sought the familiar at Groote's white-Australian town, Alyangula, 15km north of Angurugu on the west coast. The two towns lie at either end of the Rowell Highway, Groote's only major bitumen road and the artery for the island's lifeblood, the manganese ore that flows from the mine near Angurugu to the port by Alyangula.

Groote is a tropical paradise – a wonderland of long beaches, intimate coves and jagged headlands of pink sandstone. In Alyangula tropical splendours – bougainvillea, frangipani, hibiscus – hid large, almost identical elevated homes. I knew that some 1200 people, almost all mine workers, lived here, and there were boats and 4WDs everywhere – but the streets were empty. Almost everyone was indoors, air-conditioning and TV more tempting than Alyangula's beauty. As the sun dipped over Bickerton across the gulf I recalled a Leunig cartoon: mesmerised, a man watches a televised sunset, while outside the sun sets! Alyangula was beguiling but strangely soulless.

There are two worlds running on this island – the Aboriginal people and the European people with their different ways of life, 56-year-old Jambana Lalara told me with quiet authority soon after I arrived. He was right. Within a week I watched Murabuda disembowel a live turtle with a fine disregard for animal liberation niceties.

Aborigines have lived here for thousands of years. They were traditionally semi-nomadic, moving around within well-recognised clan territories living hard lives dictated by the seasons. The Aborigines, the Dreamtime and the land formed an interconnected whole, an intricate web of practical knowledge and ancient beliefs. Land and sea provided their few possessions and wholesome food: fish, turtle, dugong, wallabies and bush tucker.

Indonesian fishermen made annual voyages here in search of trepang. They introduced metal implements, tamarind trees, tobacco, cloth – and the art of dugout building, which enabled the isolated Eylandters to start travelling for war, ceremonies, marriages and trade.

$\longrightarrow$

Bernard Lalara stalks fish. His spear, made from stringy-bark, reflects generations of bush lore but his clothing speaks of Western pop culture – staple fare for Groote's youth.

Gemco, a BHP subsidiary, annually produces 15 per cent of the world's manganese which it ships from its modern port at Alyangula. The mine has a life expectancy of 50 years.

The Dutch navigator Abel Tasman named Groote Eylandt ("great island") in 1644 and Matthew Flinders charted it in 1803, but Europeans didn't disrupt the Eylandters' timeless existence until 1921, when the Church Missionary Society (CMS) built a settlement at Emerald River. In 1938, an independent community was established at Umbakumba on the ragged north-eastern coast.

Most Groote Eylandters still lived tribal lives in the 1930s, a time remembered fondly by elders today. "I loved our old life in the bush," Murabuda told me, his eyes joyful with memories. "We had a very hard life, and a lot to learn about the ceremonies, but we did it."

By the time Aunt Judith arrived in 1952, though, things had begun to change. In the comfort of her air-conditioned flat, she recalled the rigours of her early years on Groote. "A bark hut was home for nine years. There wasn't any electricity, and stores arrived three times a year by boat," she said. By then most of the Aborigines were living either at Angurugu, where the CMS mission had been relocated in 1943, or at Umbakumba. White-fella temptations – education, health services and rations – had proved too powerful, but tensions simmered between traditionally hostile clans now living cheek by jowl.

Judith had been posted to Groote as a 28-year-old school teacher, but her aim was always to record the islanders' language, Anindilyakwa. "In the holidays we went camping with the girls, and then they taught us," she recalled.

The complexities of Anindilyakwa lie stored beneath the impressive shock of white hair on Gula Lalara, Judith's long-time linguistic collaborator. "What was told us way back is written in our mind, we can't forget," Gula explained above the lapping of an incoming tide at the Angurugu River's mangrove-lined mouth.

He told me a Dreamtime story about a sawfish that swam to Groote from Bickerton Island. "Sawfish came out of the sea, started cutting his way through the island. He made the river channel, throwing the Earth aside – opening a way for him to cross the island."

Groote's ancestral storytellers could never have guessed the prophetic nature of this story. Today monstrous mechanical jaws mimic the Dreamtime sawfish.

In the mine's HQ, whirring computers disgorge critical data about ore quantity, manganese content, trace minerals and unwanted impurities. Gemco's vital statistics are impressive, the product of a highly technical operation employing about 520 people. Each week the mine's huge open cut quarries yield up to 100,000 tonnes of ore. The manganese content – about 50 per cent – is extracted by round the clock processing. Annual manganese production averages about 1.5 million tonnes, some 15 per cent of the world's total.

BHP began to evaluate the island's manganese in 1962. The Aborigines used it as a background pigment on bark paintings, but 'the Big Australian' was more interested in its industrial uses, which earned the company $41 million in 1988-89.

Four per cent of Groote was leased for mining in return for royalty payments and the company's assurances that it would protect sacred sites, rehabilitate mined areas, prohibit interference with local women and provide Aboriginal employment at award wages – then virtually unknown. Gemco, a subsidiary of BHP, was formed the following year and in March 1966 the first shipment of manganese left its shores.

Gemco's inevitable obsession with time is at odds with the islanders' laid-back attitude. In September 1989 the mine employed only 21 Aborigines, about 4 per cent of its workforce. "These Groote Eylandters are just cruising; they won't get ulcers from the nine-to-five syndrome," a white acquaintance observed somewhat enviously.

Most Aborigines seeking work look first to the Angurugu and Umbakumba councils, where clan differences and absenteeism on family business are readily accepted, but with little other non-Gemco work, there's high unemployment here.

Two weeks after I arrived, the annual clan money day – Aboriginal Christmas, as it's often called – was held at Angurugu. Clans clustered together excitedly outside the council offices in a buzz of anticipation as leaders collected their clans' cheques. Gemco pays a 1.25 per cent royalty for production above 100,000 tonnes. In 1989 the payout was

A fresh south-easterly trade wind brings white caps to the turquoise waters of Bickerton Island, 20km west of Groote Eylandt.

$1,049,000, about $870 per person, including children.

A joyful spending spree ensued. At Angurugu's store, women snapped up fridges and washing machines. Teenage boys swaggered out in flash Rambo gear while girls flirted coyly in gaudy dresses. The kids, bloated on chocolates and soft drink, pulled wheelies on shiny new BMX bikes. Mainland dealers shamelessly flogged tarted-up utes. Charter planes departed in every direction – some towards Darwin's casino.

Not all the Groote Eylandters approve of clan money. "Life is too easy for us today, too easy," said Murabuda, cuddling two grandchildren as we talked before the handout. "There's too much money here, money flowing like a river."

Gemco dangles a similar carrot to attract workers: sporting facilities, biannual leave flights, subsidised meals and supermarket prices, spacious homes – electricity, rates, the lot – for about $100 per month, a balmy climate (apart from the Wet's torrid miseries) and an environment with minimal pollution and no serious crime.

Life isn't all frangipanis for the white Australians, though. Kay Wright has lived on Groote with her husband Alan, Gemco's PR manager, since 1967. "There's always been plenty of money here, and plenty of broken marriages too," she said. Life moved indoors with air-conditioners and satellite TV and Alyangula wives without jobs or children can feel extremely isolated. Alcohol and affairs are the symptoms of lonely despair, and marriages are often sacrificed on the altar of overtime.

'Heartbreak hotel,' some Aborigines called Alyangula, dismayed by its seemingly rootless people and their obsession with money. For islanders, kin are everything. No-one is alone, everyone is part of a larger whole – the family, the clan, the land itself. Groote is indisputably Aboriginal land. Aborigines and white Australians rarely mingle here. Judith, respected by the Eylandters, has bridged the racial gulf, carried across by a desire to learn rather than teach – the common denominator of the few Europeans on Groote who mix with Aborigines.

Later that night, a crowd of yahooing teenagers wandered aimlessly around, caught between two contradictory cultures – and the despair of the elders. "I think they're saying they're bored," said Jambana as we sat beneath the tamarinds. "Surely they've got plenty things to do here, but they don't listen, you know?" The anguish of parents across Australia, it's doubly poignant among people for whom traditional life held uncompromising sanctions for even minor offences. Groote's elders had little comprehension of the mine's future size and impact in 1963, and that's the rub. Gemco has shown genuine concern for the islanders, and has exceeded its contractual obligations to promote their welfare. But no amount of goodwill can compensate for Gemco's sheer size. Today more white Australians than Aborigines live on Groote, and although the Aborigines appreciate and enjoy Gemco's benefits, many yearn for their traditional life. ■

Subject Index

◆

Index of story locations

In the series

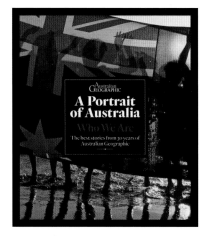
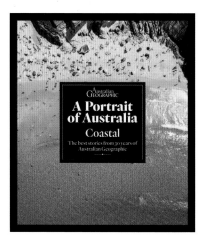
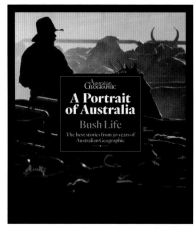
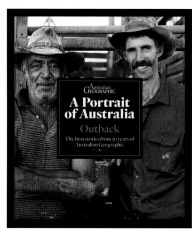

Subscribe now to
Australian Geographic
and discover even more about
Australia and its people.

 Visit   *www.magshop.com.au/australian-geographic*

or call customer service on

1300 555 176

Acknowledgements

First published in 2018

Bauer Media Ltd, 54 Park Street, Sydney, NSW 2000.

Telephone (02) 9263 9813 Fax (02) 8116 9377 Email editorial@ausgeo.com.au

www.australiangeographic.com.au

© Copyright Australian Geographic and Bauer Media

Cover image:
North Curl Curl Beach in the north of Sydney bustles with swimmers and sunbathers on the 2015 Australia Day weekend.
Photo by Andrew Gregory.

Editors Chrissie Goldrick and Karen McGhee
Chapter introductions Karen McGhee
Book designer Mike Ellott

Assistant designer Katharine McKinnon
Sub editor Josephine Sargent
Assistant commercial editor Rebecca Cotton
Commercial editor Lauren Smith
Image management Jess Teideman
Proofreader Nina Paine
Indexer Frank Povah
Print production Rachel Rae

Managing director Paul Dykzeul
Publisher specialist division Cornelia Schulze
Associate publisher, specialist division Jo Runciman
Australian Geographic editor in chief Chrissie Goldrick